PUFFIN BOOKS is part of the Penguin Random House group of companies
whose addresses can be found at global.penguinrandomhouse.com.

  Penguin
Random House
UK

First published 2018
Copyright © Victoria and Albert Museum, London, 2018
Written by Katherine Nugent
Illustrated by Margaux Carpentier
The moral right of the author and illustrator has been asserted
Printed in China   001
ISBN: 978–0–241–33986–2

Picture credits

Frida KAHLO

ARTIST ◆ WRITER ◆ ACTIVIST ◆ ICON

Discover the world of art and design through the V&A Introduces series. The Victoria and Albert Museum is the world's leading museum of art and design and houses over 2.3 million objects spanning over 5,000 years of human creativity. Inspired by its exhibitions, collections and heroes, this collectable series brings the wonder of the designed world to all!

'I am my own muse.
I am the subject
I know best.
The subject I want
to better.'

Frida Kahlo

Fridamania

Frida Kahlo was a rule breaker. One of the most famous
artists of the twentieth century, she was a revolutionary
spirit, an incredible painter and a powerful woman who was
not afraid to be herself. Frida's life was filled with hardship,
but she took her physical pain and emotional struggle and
turned them into extraordinary works of art.

From her striking self-portraits to her bold sense of fashion,
Frida always expressed herself honestly and unapologetically.
She made up her own rules. Frida redefined what it meant
to be a woman and created her own ideals of beauty. She was
proud of Mexican culture and had a firm belief in equality
for all people, regardless of class, gender, race or religion.

Today, Frida's passion for life continues to inspire artists and
trailblazers all around the world. Her legacy is so powerful
that it has even been given a name: 'Fridamania'.

Young Frida

Frida Kahlo was born on 6 July 1907 in the beautiful borough of Coyoacán, Mexico City, the third of four sisters. When she was only six years old, she caught polio and had to spend nine months mostly alone in her bedroom. Frida recovered but, because of the disease, her right leg was weak and thin for the rest of her life.

Frida as a child. She was named after the German word for peace, 'friede'

Guillermo Kahlo

Although Frida was raised in a strong female household (she called her mother her 'chief'!), Frida's father held a very special place in her heart. Born in the German Empire, Wilhelm Kahlo was nineteen when he moved to Mexico and changed his name to Guillermo. He encouraged Frida to take part in sports like football and wrestling to strengthen her weak leg – these were very unusual activities for a girl at the time!

Guillermo was a professional photographer

School years

Guillermo had big dreams for Frida. When she was fourteen, he enrolled her in one of the best schools in the country – Escuela Nacional Preparatoria. Frida was one of only 35 girls among 2,000 students! She was fascinated by biology and hoped to become a doctor one day. At school, Frida showed off her rebellious spirit and became part of the 'Cachuchas', a cheeky group of friends who loved playing pranks. One of the members was Alejandro Gomez Arias, Frida's boyfriend.

REVOLUCION MEXICANA

Although Frida had a mixed heritage, both Mexican and European, she loved Mexico and was proud of her country. As a young student in the years following the Mexican Revolution, Frida was part of an exciting movement to create a new national identity for Mexico, one that returned to true 'Mexicanism' and moved away from European influences. Frida saw herself as being so closely connected to her native country that, when she was older, she would say she was born three years later – so that her birth year matched the start of the Mexican Revolution.

The accident

On 17 September 1925, eighteen-year-old Frida was travelling on a bus with her boyfriend, Alejandro, when it crashed into a tram. A metal handrail pierced Frida's torso and she suffered many painful injuries, including a broken spinal column. It was a miracle that she survived the terrible accident and it changed her life forever – although she didn't realize it at the time, her injuries meant she couldn't have children, which was devastating for Frida.

Frida and her boyfriend were on their way home to Coyoacán

During her recovery, Frida couldn't leave her bed so she began to paint to pass the time. Her mother ordered a specially made easel, which would allow Frida to paint while lying down. Using a mirror attached to her bed, Frida began to paint self-portraits and discovered her talent for art.

Frida spent three months recovering from her injuries

Diego Rivera

Frida first met the famous Mexican painter Diego Rivera when she started at Escuela Preparatoria, where he was painting murals. In 1928, after she had recovered from the accident, Frida asked Diego whether he thought she could make a living as an artist. Frida deeply admired Diego and he found her brilliant and beautiful.

The two artists quickly fell in love and were married on 21 August 1929. Frida was twenty years younger than Diego and her mother compared their wedding to one between a dove and an elephant!

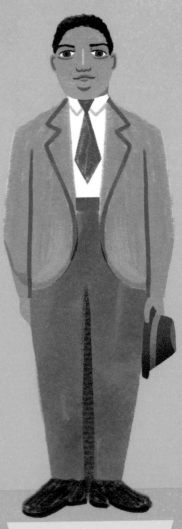

A photograph of Frida painting a self-portrait, with Diego Rivera

★ A new home ★

In 1930, a year into their marriage, the couple moved to the United States where Diego, a famous artist in America, had been invited to create several murals. Frida also dedicated herself to her art. Her portrait 'Frieda and Diego Riviera' was included in an exhibition in San Francisco in 1931. It was her first painting to be shown to the public.

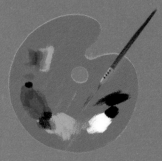

Frida and Diego at an art exhibition in New York

Diego was content in America, but Frida was homesick. She missed Mexico, its people, architecture and rich culture. The self-portrait below shows Frida standing between the two countries holding a Mexican flag, which reveals where her loyalties lie. To her right, Mexico is represented as an ancient temple. To her left, America is represented as a factory, billowing smoke clouds into the sky.

'Self-portrait on the Borderline Between Mexico and the United States'

In 1933, Frida and Diego finally moved back to Mexico. After some difficult years, they divorced in 1939 but remarried less than a year later in December 1940 and moved back into Frida's childhood home, La Casa Azul.

La Casa Azul

The Blue House

La Casa Azul can be considered one of Frida's works of art. The house was originally white but was given a Mexican 'makeover' when Frida moved there with Diego in 1940. They painted it in deep blue and coral and decorated it with sculptures, paintings and trinkets that showcased their love for Mexican culture.

While the entire home is dazzling, the kitchen was Frida's pride and joy. Painted bright yellow and electric blue, Frida decorated the walls with small pots arranged to spell out her name.

Frida found peace and comfort in her garden at La Casa Azul. There she would relax on her patio, tend to her plants and play with her many pets, including Fulang-Chang, her spider monkey, and Granizo, her fawn. Brimming with colourful native flowers, the garden was a paradise that inspired many of her paintings.

Her garden even acted as an open-air classroom where she would invite her art students when her health problems prevented her from leaving her home.

Frida Kahlo in her garden at La Casa Azul, 1951

Frida the fashionista

Frida Kahlo was a fearless fashionista! She used clothing to proudly show off her identity as a strong, independent Mexican woman.

The traditional *Tehuana* dress became a bit like a uniform for Frida.

1. Headpiece

Frida loved to wear her hair in braids, which she arranged in unique styles. She would weave brightly coloured fabric into them and decorate her hair with flowers to create a stunning crown.

2. Huipil

Frida would wear square-cut, loose-fitting blouses called *huipiles*.

Underneath her long skirts, Frida wore a lace underskirt called an *enagua*. The bottom of the *enagua* would peek out beneath the skirt.

The dress is made up of three parts . . .

Disability and dress

Fashion let Frida transform her body into a work of art. When Frida had to wear plaster casts to support her spine, which was damaged in the bus accident, she decorated the casts with drawings of tigers, monkeys and birds. Later in life, when she had to have her weak right leg amputated, she designed a beautiful red-leather platform shoe for her prosthetic leg.

'Memory' or 'The Heart', 1937

What did Frida paint?

Frida's art was very personal and, of the 143 paintings she did in her lifetime, 55 were self-portraits. Through her work, she vividly expressed her immense physical and emotional suffering. A local critic once said, 'Her paintings are her biography'.

'Memory', 'The Heart'

Frida's emotional heartache was the subject of many paintings. In a work from 1937, 'Memory' or 'The Heart', Frida depicts herself crying with no arms, standing between her *Tehuana* dress and her school uniform. The painting represents her struggle to find an identity without Diego. Her large heart lies on the floor and two cupids sit on either end of the rod that pierces her chest, symbolizing the pain that love has caused her.

Nature and animals

Frida was a true nature lover. She adored plants and animals and this shone through her work. She had many beloved pets, including monkeys, dogs, birds and a fawn, and often included them in her paintings. The animals always played an important symbolic role and their meanings were often influenced by Mexican folklore.

In one painting, 'The Wounded Deer', Frida depicts herself as having the body of a deer. She used her pet fawn, Granizo, as her model.

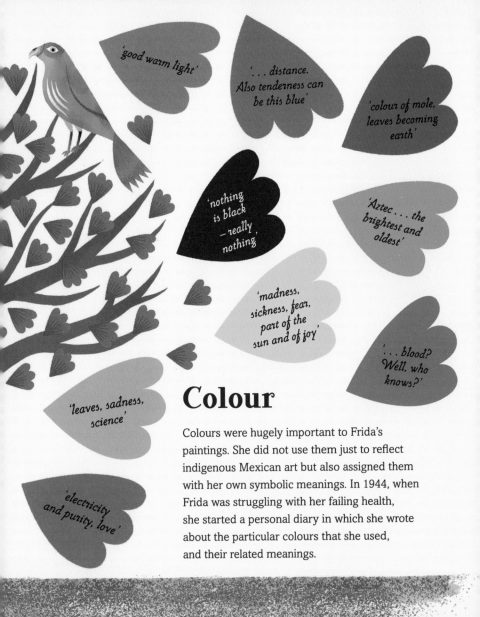

'good warm light'

'...distance. Also tenderness can be this blue'

'colour of mole, leaves becoming earth'

'nothing is black — really nothing'

'Aztec...the brightest and oldest'

'madness, sickness, fear, part of the sun and of joy'

'...blood? Well, who knows?'

'leaves, sadness, science'

'electricity and purity, love'

Colour

Colours were hugely important to Frida's paintings. She did not use them just to reflect indigenous Mexican art but also assigned them with her own symbolic meanings. In 1944, when Frida was struggling with her failing health, she started a personal diary in which she wrote about the particular colours that she used, and their related meanings.

◆ Symbolism ◆

'Self-Portrait with Monkeys' is one of Frida's many paintings that uses nature and animals as powerful symbols. It was painted during a very busy time for Frida, when she was teaching at the National School of Painting, Sculpture and Printmaking in Mexico City in 1943.

Spider monkeys

Although monkeys are symbols of desire in Mexican mythology, here Frida uses them to represent her four most devoted students. She called them 'Los Fridos'. Frida stands among them, proud and protective.

Bird of paradise

This flower represents freedom and joy. It may be a symbol of the happiness and 'paradise' that Frida found when teaching her loyal students.

Green leaves

According to Frida's colour wheel, green represents 'sadness'. The brightly coloured bird of paradise and the protective way the spider monkeys surround her could symbolize the joy that teaching brought Frida in a time of emotional pain.

Viva la Frida

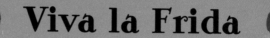

In 1953, Frida's health took a turn for the worse and her right leg had to be amputated from the knee. Despite moments of feeling hopeless, Frida continued to paint and her last work is a proud display of her refusal to be defeated. Frida chose to paint a still life of watermelons, a popular symbol in Mexican culture that is associated with the celebration of death. A week before she died, Frida wrote the words '*Viva la Vida*' on the piece, meaning '*Long Live Life*'.

Frida's wardrobe

After her death in 1954, Diego locked a cupboard of Frida's possessions in a bathroom at La Casa Azul. He demanded that it remain locked until fifteen years after his death. When the room was finally opened in 2004, it revealed a treasure trove of around 300 of Frida's most beloved things! From yellow cat-eye sunglasses to painted body casts, the pieces gave an incredible insight into Frida's life and helped establish her as a legendary artist and icon.

Frida's legacy

Frida Kahlo was a trailblazing force who expressed herself honestly and proudly in everything she did. Her legacy as a rule breaker and an inspirational artist continues to make its mark in the world today.

The revolutionary

Frida's determination to follow her own path in life, her commitment to her personal beliefs and her bravery in the face of hardship has established her as an inspirational icon.

The artist

Frida's art continues to inspire all kinds of artists today. The lead singer of Coldplay, Chris Martin, even took inspiration from Frida's final painting when writing the number one hit, 'Viva La Vida'.

The trendsetter

Frida's unique sense of dress is just as influential today as her art. Inspiring designers such as Jean-Paul Gaultier and celebrities like Beyoncé, Frida's style is always being reproduced in popular culture.

The icon

Frida's self-portraits have earned her the nickname, 'Mother of the Selfie'. Her image is considered a work of art in itself and can be found on all sorts of memorabilia, from mugs to T-shirts.

Life story

1907

Frida is born on 6 July in Coyoacán, Mexico City.

1926

Paints her first self-portrait, 'Self-Portrait in a Velvet Dress'.

1913

Diagnosed with polio at the age of six.

1922

Starts school at the National Preparatory School in Mexico City.

1925

Miraculously survives a tram accident. Bedridden, Frida starts to paint to pass the time.

Other important events in Frida's lifetime

1910 – Start of the Mexican Revolution

1910 – Salvador Dali's first painting was completed

1929

Marries Diego Rivera in a civil ceremony.

1937

Frida's work is first publicly exhibited in Mexico.

1939

Diego and Frida officially divorce on 6 November.

1938

Goes to New York for her first solo exhibition.

1954

Dies on 13 July in her bed at La Casa Azul.

1940

Remarries Diego on 8 December. The couple move into La Casa Azul.

1953

Frida's first solo exhibition in Mexico.

1914 – Start of the First World War

1929 – Start of the Great Depression in America

1939 – Start of the Second World War

1940s – Start of the 'Mexican Miracle' years